A FIELD GUIDE
TO WRITING FICTION

By the same author

The Big Sky
The Way West
Fair Land, Fair Land:
These Thousand Hills
Arfive
The Last Valley
Big Sky, Fair Land:
The Environmental Essays of A. B. Guthrie, Jr.
(edited by David Petersen)
Once Upon a Pond (for children)
Four Miles from Ear Mountain (poems)

MYSTERIES

Wild Pitch
The Genuine Article
No Second Wind
Playing Catch-Up
Murder in the Cotswolds

A
FIELD GUIDE
TO WRITING
FICTION

A. B. Guthrie, Jr.

HarperCollins*Publishers*

A FIELD GUIDE TO WRITING FICTION. Copyright © 1991 by A. B. Guthrie, Jr., and
Carol B. Guthrie. All rights reserved. Printed in the United States of America. No
part of this book may be used or reproduced in any manner whatsoever without
written permission except in the case of brief quotations embodied in critical articles
and reviews. For information address HarperCollins Publishers, 10 East 53rd Street,
New York, NY 10022.

FIRST EDITION

Designed by Barbara DuPree Knowles

LIBRARY OF CONGRESS CATALOGING-IN-PUBLICATION DATA

Guthrie, A. B. (Alfred Bertram), 1901–
  A field guide to writing fiction / A. B. Guthrie, Jr.—1st ed.
    p. cm.
  ISBN 0-06-270002-2
  1. Fiction—Authorship.   I. Title.
PN3355.G88 1991
808.3—dc20   90-55537

91 92 93 94 95 CC/HC 10 9 8 7 6 5 4 3 2 1

To Young Writers
as a partial and indirect discharge of my indebtedness
for help from old friends whom I could not
and cannot repay in any coin

Contents

Contents

Contents

Contents

x

A FIELD GUIDE
TO WRITING FICTION

Introduction

FOR MORE THAN FORTY YEARS I have made my living by
writing alone—novels, short stories, magazine pieces, poems,
and screenplays. I have had no inheritance to draw on, no
salaried positions, no grants, no income whatever except what
my writing has earned.

Here I put down, as concisely as I can manage, what I have
learned through effort, trial and error, association, rejection,
and acceptance. I endorse a certain method or style of fiction
writing. Other authors have employed other methods successfully. Fair enough. What works works, as Theodore Morrison
often said. I would add a clause to it: What works works, but
what works best works better.

I have attended many writers' conferences and listened to
many a speaker. I have read a good many books having to do
with the craft. But nowhere have I found a short and useful
body of instruction. As an eager novice, I didn't need lengthy
discussions of mood, theme, symbolism, and other abstractions. I wanted guidance. I wanted the nuts and bolts of creative composition, the structure on which to build, with
suggestions as to the building.

Some of the books about fiction can be helpful, make no
mistake about that. Some, like DeVoto's *The World of Fiction,*

deal admirably with points of view, but in a manner more helpful to semi-pros than to beginning or would-be writers. Kempton's *The Short Story* is very good but limited as the title shows. It's hard to find these days. Brooks and Warren have some good things to say, but my remembrance is that they help readers more than they help writers.

The best book of its kind, the best that I've encountered, is John Gardner's *The Art of Fiction.* But Gardner, in addition to being a good writer, was a highly regarded teacher. He draws on his classroom experience and goes far more into detail than there is room for here. Plot and rhythm, for instance, and theme, symbolism, and other subjects. Beginners of fiction believe that plot is the end and all of creative writing, but my experience is that plots, somewhat like themes, develop of themselves if the writer has a story clearly in mind. Rhythm will come if the writer has any ear at all. The hazy subjects I won't touch on. They've been done often enough.

If on occasion I use lines from my own work as illustrations, it is not because they are superior but because they are mine and ready to hand.

Sometimes I may speak in the first person plural, for in my ears as I write are the friendly bits of advice given me by Theodore Morrison, William Sloane, Bernard DeVoto, and Robert Frost, all dead now but often speaking through me. To the late Professor Morrison I owe an especial debt. We once talked about writing a book for beginning writers but got only so far as to develop some maxims.

Bear in mind that I am addressing myself not to people who want to write but to those who will write or are writing. Too often I encounter men and women, young and old, who speak of the wish to write and the intention of doing so sometime. They populate the meadows of forlorn hopes.

So here is what I have learned through association and long practice. Here are what I consider the fundamentals of good fiction writing. Here are the nitty-grittys, with illustrations, offered as helps to beginning writers and perhaps teachers of creative writing. Here are the nuts and bolts, to be built on or rejected as students and teachers choose.

Good luck to all.

ONE

The Big Three:
Scene, Description, and
Summary

FOR PURPOSES OF STUDY, fiction has been divided into three parts—scene, description, and summary.

The distinction is butchery, for fiction is of a piece. Vivisection is justified only for convenience and for the moment.

Scene is just what the name suggests. It is drama. It is people and things in action. The dramatist speaks of characters being "on scene," of leaving and entering it. It may serve you well in writing to think of the playhouse, remembering, though, that you are not confined to a playhouse stage. The outdoors is there if you need it.

Description is description. It is the portrayal of surroundings, landscapes or interiors, weather, human features, reactions, and dress. But don't throw it in just because you feel it is time for a bit of it. It must be related to the sentiments, conversation, appearances, and perceptions of your characters, to one or more of these elements.

Beginners often find difficulty in this integration. So, an example:

"I won't be seeing you again very soon," his father said. He picked a grass stem and nibbled on it while his gaze went east, across the little town a half mile below them, perhaps to the cemetery on the hill beyond. The graves of three of his loved ones lay there, the marble head-stones catching dim glints from the late sun.

"Now, now, it will be soon," Hugh answered, know-ing that never again lay in their parting. Never again. Sadness was in him. The declining sun was making for a notch in the mountains, about ready to say goodbye to the world. "No, Dad," he said, knowing better. "We'll see each other again soon."

Here we have conversation, mood, and description all joined. They are of a piece. The description is not tossed in as a separate bit of narrative. It belongs where it is.

Summary is transition. It is the bridging of gaps in which little or nothing happens to the onward time in which some-thing does. It involves a change in time, a change of circum-stances, and perhaps of cast. And it can be damn difficult to deal with, tedious to both writer and reader unless done very well. You may find you have no need to summarize. If your story flows right along, one episode after another in sequence, there'll be no idle time to account for.

When you do have to bridge unimportant time, and change scene and characters, don't fret unduly. There's a sim-ple way. It's the white-space break. It prepares the reader for a shift. No tedious words necessary.

A new chapter will do the same thing, but I use chapters more sparingly. I use them when the story arrives at a momen-tary stay and gives the reader pause. To use them arbitrarily in place of white-space breaks is to clutter your story with chapter headings.

There's a maxim that the good writer does everything at once, that he combines scene, summary, and description. Sometimes he may be able to do so as in this illustration:

"We been ridin' this same range for six months," Bill said, shifting in the saddle. He squinted up at the sky, where the sun burned hot as a blister.

Here are description and summary, all placed within scene. But seldom is the going so easy. When it becomes difficult, remember the white-space break, and praise the Lord.

TWO

Viewpoint: Ways to Tell a Story

Y OU HAVE A CHOICE, and a choice within choices, in writing a story, short or book-length.

The first and perhaps easiest is to write in the first person. "I" or "we" gives the story an immediate intimacy that "he" or "they" does not.

But there are options even here. In one your "I" may be the protagonist, in the other the witness; in other words, to be the doer or the witness to another's doings. If your character is the doer, you must guard against making him too heroic, too full of himself, or too boastful. But if you make him too retiring, you run the risk of creating a wimp.

A sort of bastard form enters here, neither first-person nor third. It's the fly-on-the-wall method. Nothing is narrated in it but what the camera can see and the recorder hear. It is infrequently used. Hemingway's "The Killers" is perhaps the best example.

Second-person stories are rare and more rarely good. The constant "you" gets tiresome.

So to third-person stories, and a choice in the matter of viewpoint—whether to write as the author omniscient, which puts the author on the page, or the author subjective, which limits perceptions to the immediate-viewpoint character, that is, to the character who is feeling, seeing, and hearing in a given passage.

The author omniscient knows everything. He can flit from one man's mind to another's. He can make his own comments on person, place, and predicament. As it pleases him, he can see importances that his characters cannot. He is not far in this respect from the old-time author who was fond of saying, "Dear reader, more trouble is in store for our people," or "Had they but known . . . " In short, the author plays God.

I go the other way. I don't want the author coming between me and his characters. I don't like the author on the page. Let the buttinsky get off. I speak from a long-time dislike. As a boy I hated to see the word *book* in a story I was reading. It reminded me I had a book in my hand. It erased my illusion.

Gardner refers to a couple of very good writers who wrote as omniscients. That's proof enough for him. He doesn't speculate or wonder how their works would have turned out had they not been all-knowing.

Ford Madox Ford, a distinguished writer, said, "The object of the novelist is to keep the reader entirely oblivious of the fact that the author exists—even of the fact that he is holding a book."

That conviction, it's needless to emphasize, stands directly opposed to Gardner's preference.

Thomas Hardy plays God in *Tess of the D'Urbervilles*. When Tess dies at Stonehenge after a pitiful and tragic life, Hardy concludes, "Justice was done, and the President of the Immortals, in the Aeschylean phrase, had had his sport with Tess."

News to us, huh? We didn't know, even after reading of the blind cruelties of fate, that Tess had had a sorry time. No, indeed. Hardy has to tell us how pitiful and tragic her life had been. And he has to go on and on, laying it on thick. He beats us with words. We have to lie prone and bleeding to realize the full measure of tragedy.

For all that, Hardy was a great and powerful writer, and *Tess* is a great book. I just wish Hardy had given me and other readers some credit for imagination.

The Battle of the Little Bighorn, sometimes known as Custer's Last Stand, can be used as illustrations of viewpoint.

Omniscience would have the chronicler flitting all over the battlefield. As God, it would take us on a guided tour. Starting with Custer and the main body of his troops, we might visit Reno down in the valley, perhaps already hard-pressed by the Indians, then on to Benteen and the supply train, some distance from immediate danger, then back to Custer and the charging redskins. The reporter might dip into Custer's mind, seeing a dawning awareness of defeat there, of his probable death and the death of his troopers, and all his dreams of glory done to death.

Indeed, this method might give us an excellent report, but a report it would be, with the author always between us and the battle, putting us always at a remove from the immediate.

By contrast, the third-person subjective:

He dismounted and handed the reins to a horse holder, as other men were doing. He went forward, lay on his stomach, legs spread, his loaded Springfield held just ahead of him. "Let them come," he said to himself. "No reason to fear." Hands steady now. Custer's words rang in his head. One trooper was the equal of a dozen red devils. That's what he said, and the general ought to know.

There were sounds around him, men shifting positions, checking their rifles, one saying, "Let the red sons of bitches come. Ready here, Sitting Bull."

And here they came, hundreds of them, thousands, mounted and shouting out of painted faces, their colors flashing in the sun. He drew a breath, feeling his rectum tighten, and took aim with the Springfield. Hold it! Hold it! Then on order he fired, and saw an Indian slump. He pulled back the bolt and saw the ejector slide over the rim of the cartridge casing. No time to gouge it out. He sprang to his feet, his rifle reversed in his hands, ready as a club. The man next to him was on his feet, then he folded with a grunt and lay still. He caught a glimpse of troopers running, the mounted Indians hot after them, and there was Custer surrounded. He caught that glimpse and no more, for horses snorted and reared around him, and yells came from painted faces, and raised arms held battle axes.

He swung the butt of his rifle and hit a wild head, and the Indian fell sprawling. Then his own head exploded, lights flashing in it, and he felt himself going down, the lights dying.

From that trooper, after a white-space break, we may move to Reno, then, after a break, to Benteen, from him to Custer or perhaps some other characters. In each white-space section, we'll be inside one man's mind. We'll be limited to what he sees, feels, and experiences.

And we'll have immediacy. We'll be next to the characters, not separated by a reporting intelligence, and the reader's emotional experience will be the greater.

Do not shift viewpoint within a scene. The change comes preferably after a white-space break or the beginning of a new chapter. In shifting viewpoint make it plain early on that a different intelligence has taken over.

And I insist that here is the better method, even agreeing that breaks are authorial contrivances. The reader won't mind or be bothered by an intrusive translator, and he won't have to endure sermons.

POSTSCRIPT: John Steinbeck combines the two styles and does so successfully. In the beginning, as the all-knowing author, he sets the scene and tells something of the situation and the characters. That done, he ceases to play God and lets his characters act and speak without his intrusion.

THREE

Show, Don't Tell

T WO MAXIMS:

1. Show, don't tell.
2. The task of fiction is to excite, not to imprison the imagination of the reader.

Enscribe these bits of advice on your skull. They are all-important, more important than anything else that may appear in this booklet.

And while they are important, they are most difficult of all to apply without lapse. Even the seasoned author often will find he has fallen from grace and must atone.

The two maxims are combined here because of their close relationship. If you show, rather than tell, you will excite the reader's imagination. Conversely, if you excite that imagination, it will be by showing.

Again and again in these pages you will find references and allusions to these bits of advice, and illustrations applied elsewhere are applicable here.

Ernest Hemingway provides an instructive example in "The Short Happy Life of Francis Macomber."

Macomber, shamed for having fled before the charge of

a lion, later finds courage and stands resolute as a swamp buffalo charges him. His wife, behind him, fires her rifle, maybe at the buffalo, and by accident or design shoots Macomber in the back of the head. The force of the bullet knocks him face down. The wife and the white hunter run to the body. Here the amateur writer would have had a great time describing what a mess of head and face the bullet made on emerging. Instead, Hemingway has the white hunter say, "I wouldn't turn him over."

What a spur to the reader! His imagination takes wing. He doesn't need imprisoning words. His imagination soars above all the adjectives and enforcing phrases of verbal resources.

FOUR

Characters

CHARACTERS MAKE THE STORY, short or long. They are
the indispensable element. Without them there is nothing.
And they must be alive, present, distinctive, essential to mood
and movement.

Every story is the story of a man or a woman or a small
group of people. They may be in agreement or disagreement.
Surrounding them are the minor characters, some supportive
of the principals or one of the principals, the others opposed.
No matter what else they are, they must be alive. To make
one of your characters the epitome of evil and another the
epitome of virtue is to portray cardboard characters. Man is a
mixture of good and bad qualities. The gentle man can be
violent, the violent man gentle. It is the proportion of these
qualities, one to another, that constitute the individual's nature.

It often happens with me that characters walk on the page,
rather to my surprise. They proceed to grow, become in-
dividuals, and assert themselves. They have ideas, manner-
isms, motives, and crochets of their own.

Drive them with a loose rein. Give them freedom, but
within limits, else they'll take over your story.

The buds of qualities we are likely to think foreign to us
exist in everyone. If you are in the mind of a person of the

opposite sex, you can be that person if you try hard enough. You can think as he or she thinks. You can react as he or she would react, think like one or the other and experience that person's trials. You can be dark-minded and violent or meek and long-suffering, while allowing for contrary turns of temperament.

I call this ability to waken the buds in us the final feat of the imagination in fiction.

If you introduce a character by name alone and return to him later on, again by name alone, the reader will ask, "Now who in hell is this joker?" He'll be vexed if he has to turn back to find out.

To avoid this confusion, give the character at the outset some distinguishing feature of body or habit of speech. Give him a blazing red head or a squint. Give her an engaging or wistful or grim appearance or a figure as delicate as a faun's. Give her something distinctive.

Later in your story, when the character comes on scene again, you can identify him or her by some reference to oddities, by some glancing reminder.

The reader will be grateful, if not realizing what for.

With luck, then, your characters will develop almost of themselves without pressing assistance from you. They may say and do unexpected things. That will be good. It will make them realer. It will expand them as personages. But be careful here. You may not make or let your characters do violence to their fundamental natures. If by action or word a character proves himself unscrupulous or vicious, so be it. Allow him whatever good qualities he has, but remember, no matter the soft yet cynical assertion that to understand all is to forgive all—a son of a bitch remains a son of a bitch. No sawdust trail for him. No being born again. At bottom he is what he has proved himself to be.

Surface impressions are a different matter. They can be wrong. You may want to change them.

I cite a case from my own experience. I was on vacation from my job in Kentucky and spending two or three days at a dude ranch in the south fork of the Teton River in Montana. The rancher had been having trouble with black bears that broke into vacant cabins and the chilling room where he kept meat for the table. He complained to authorities, and they sent out a professional. He was baiting and setting traps just behind the main lodge when I arrived.

We had dinner and waited as dark descended. The hunter, a trim and muscled young man, showed me his new rifle. It was all blued metal and shiny stock. Carefully he wiped hand prints from the barrel. That rifle, he told me, was big enough for any animal on the continent. Or any other, I thought as he sat admiring its killing power.

It was dark now, and all of a sudden there came a banging in back of the lodge. The hunter grabbed up his rifle. I followed him and the beam of his flashlight. We rounded the corner of the building, and there was the bear, standing on his hind legs, trying to free himself from the legtrap by beating it against a pine. Seeing us, he lowered himself. In the flashlight's gleam I could see the glaze in his eyes, the fearful, belligerent gaze.

The hunter knelt and, holding the flash under the barrel of the rifle, took careful aim. The blast of the shot shattered the silence. The bear collapsed.

"Hold on," the hunter said to me. "We'll wait to make sure he's dead." His voice sounded grim, not exultant as I would have expected.

Then he stepped forward and put his hand on the bear as he looked. The shot had burst the bear's skull.

The hunter looked away. I could see the hard outline of

his young face in the glow of the flashlight. He touched the bear again and shook his head and said to himself and me and the universe, "Goddamn such a job anyhow!"

. . .

Just one more thing about characters—the reflective character.

Often you get best effect in describing a character's appearance or reaction by having a side character speak. An example recently came to my attention. It's from Carter Dickson's *My Late Wives.* Here a detective, after a rather general conversation, says, "Now, now, miss . . . no call to go and get alarmed." Before he spoke, the reader hadn't realized she was upset. Now it has come to him full force.

Another example: Here's our protagonist, frightened before a locked door. He has the key in his hand but hesitates, shrinking. We can go on and make his fright real enough, but make it even realer by having a side character intervene, saying, "Hey, man, what's wrong? You look like it's a roomful of ghosts. Here, give me that key."

FIVE

Characters and Solitude

IF YOU LEAVE your character solitary for a length of time, you'd better question yourself.

Fiction is people acting and reacting to each other, to the forces and choices and challenges that confront them.

Example:

Joe woke in a strange bed, in a room that seemed to rock as he watched. His head rocked with it. Jesus, his poor head. Would he never learn? His hands explored weakly. He wasn't even undressed. He was lying, fully clothed, on top of the covers. He tried to think how he had got here.

It had started yesterday afternoon, or maybe morning, in a saloon called Joe's Place. He could remember that much. There were other saloons and more drinks that he bought and his new-found pals drank with him.

And then the girl. Red-headed, wasn't she? A hooker, wasn't she? He put his hand to his head as bits and pieces of last night came to mind. A hooker? Anyhow, she was ready to come upstairs with him, and there was trouble in the lobby. He felt his forehead. Hadn't someone hit him? Hadn't they carried him up here and thrown him in bed?

The small-town guy in the city. That was him. And Mabel had warned him back there at home, and, thinking of her, he began to cry.

At this point we have had enough of Joe and his musings. How to put him on scene? How to get some life into the story? Example:

Joe stirred. Someone was knocking somewhere. If he kept still, maybe the knocking would stop. But it came again, harder this time.

He rolled out of bed, lurching, and put his hand on the wall for support, astonished to find he was dressed. "Minute," he said, his voice hoarse in his ears.

A man stood at the door, a squat, hard-faced man who said, "Get out."

"Get out? I got money. I paid."

"Get out!" The man stepped forward.

"I don't—don't get it."

"Lucky you're not in the drunk tank. You can thank me for that."

"Who are you, anyhow?"

"House detective. Get out or here come the cops."

The room swam to the man's words.

We are on scene here. We are in the present, with men speaking and reacting, not lost in some hazy past where even remembrance is dim.

But hold on here. How about Hemingway's *Old Man and the Sea?* For most of that story the old man is alone. The difference is that he is not passive. Forces are working on him, and he is responding. The sea rolls around him, the great fish fights the line, the sharks snatch chunks from the fish when finally it is brought alongside. The old man has no time for regrets or recollections. He's too busy. In a sense he is not solitary, for there are the sea, the fish, and the sharks, characters in themselves.

SIX

Characters
and Compassion

Y EARS AGO I stumbled on a brief, blue-paper–bound pamphlet written and published by an aging Indiana preacher who had traveled the Oregon Trail with a fur brigade in 1841–42. He went penniless, uncomplaining, secure in the belief that God would provide. Indeed, He seems to have done so, for Joseph Williams, the preacher, arrived safely in Oregon. There, to earn money, he worked in a pit, sawing into planks the logs above him. Strenuous toil for anybody, but though he was sixty-four years old, he didn't whine. It was God's will that he work thus.

Brother Williams believed in a personal God, a close-at-hand God who tallied good deeds and bad and dealt or would deal accordingly. Williams grieved over the sinful ways of his companions and called down heaven's mercy and wrath.

But it was the Deists and Deism he inveighed against most. That wicked idea, to reject supernatural revelation and contend that nature proved the existence of God, as well as His indifference to His creations!

Now, when I began thinking about the Oregon trail and a story subsequently called *The Way West,* it struck me as good that I should include Brother Williams in the westbound party. Boy, I thought, will I have fun with this simplistic soul, this Hoosier redneck whose God rode the nearest cloud, thunderbolt in hand. I'd horse him around, I'd hold him to ridicule, I'd show him for what he was, a lame-brain believer.

But I found I couldn't do it. He was such a simple, honest, uncomplaining man. I grew to like him, to admire him for his sincere and abiding faith, if not for his intellect. So I renamed him Brother Weatherby and let him be himself. No use to ask that God be with him. His God was.

Moral: It is not the business of the novelist to burlesque characters. If they are funny, let them be funny in their own way, not by authorial manipulation or exaggeration. For the writing of novels, even humorous novels, is a serious business. To make a travesty out of a character is to present no character at all.

Outlines and Plots

I HAVE SHIED AWAY from outlines and said in my introduction that I'd give plot short shrift. But I must say something about both.

Many successful writers do outline their stories before beginning the actual writing. Some do it in detail, incident by incident and chapter by chapter. I have never done so, feeling that outlines would constrict me, limiting me to what I had planned. They could be obstacles to an imagination that might flourish as the story progressed.

I usually start out with just a few characters, maybe only two, never more than five. They may be of different sexes or the same sex, according to the needs of the story. They must vary in attitude, outlook and purpose. In the group will be my protagonist. The characters introduced, I let them go. I give them all the freedom I can within the limits of my plan. Plan? Yes, plan, but not outline. I usually know where my story will go and how it will end. But as the characters assume individuality, as the story builds almost of itself, I find fresh incidents, new descriptions, enlarged thrust in the telling.

I suppose in a loose sense this could be called plotting, but it is plotting of the moment.

I have written, with modest success, a number of mystery

or detective stories. Here again I know the overall picture and I have the culprit in mind. The secret here, if it is a secret, is to give the innocents some reason for violence while slyly involving the culprit. The end should come as a sort of "of course" development, one plain to see once exposed. I shake my head over mysteries that require a final, long chapter of explanation that discloses the detective's line of reasoning.

EIGHT

Dialogue

FICTIONAL DIALOGUE is not like the actual conversation of people, although, well done, it seems real. People talk is wordy, discursive, off the point, disjointed. Fiction foreshortens what people would say. It ignores the irrelevant. It goes somewhere, in the direction the author chooses. Idle words are omitted, unless by chance they illuminate a character, when they become not idle at all.

A court case serves as an example. The minutes of the trial, with all the legalisms, the questions that seem to be pointless, would make dull reading. So the author, writing of the trial, chooses what is important, what really relates to the issue, forgetting all the rest.

The beginning writer may fear that the simple *say* used in quoted conversation will grow tiresome by repetition. The reader will accept it readily.

Yet there are ways to avoid it if you wish. If a character has an oddity of speech, use it. No *said* needed. Another way is to write that the speaker gestured or frowned or whatever and follow immediately with his quoted words.

But don't fear to say *said*.

NINE

Internal Monologue

HERE THE FICTION WRITER has a great advantage over the playwright, who can never get inside a character's head but must indicate his feelings by speech or word. The playwright used to use asides by way of explanation, as if the fellow actors could not hear what he said to the audience. Another method was the over-voice from offstage.

Neither method compares to internal monologue as a vehicle for private thought.

Internal monologue is not difficult to manage if you are firmly planted in a character's mind. Often, when you are, it is not even necessary to report "he thought" to identify the thinker.

Suppose we are in the mind of a United States senator who is being offered a bribe. During a long tenure the senator has won a reputation for integrity. The very notion of a bribe offends him. Then, in the mind of the senator:

Hear the man out. Bear with the bastard just long enough. Then jolt him with the idea that some men could not be bought. Prove it to him. Kick his ass out.

Internal monologue is the silent talk of a character to himself. It is an expression of his inner feelings unuttered but turning in his mind.

TEN

Knowing Your Subject

ADVISERS ARE LIKELY to say, "Write what you know about." That's good, if to me limited, counsel. It seems to imply that the author must have had personal experience with everything in his story, that he must have a personal familiarity with the houses he writes about, with the contours and character of the land, with the streets of the cities, with the concerns of men.

I would change that bit of advice to read: Know what you write about. Through study and research you can gain accurate knowledge of older times. You can write a historical novel. The combination of personal experience and research opens all doors.

Examples of insufficient research are abundant. A good many years ago a novelist of some note—perhaps because she was beautiful and wrote about sex—described a horse-drawn carriage as "handsome." Interviewed later, she said she didn't know anything about carriages and thought the adjective she used was description enough. Perhaps it was, but I would want to know that this handsome vehicle carried kerosene sidelights, their burners enclosed in ornate wrought iron and beveled plate glass. I would want to know, too, that the body of it rode not on springs but on heavy leather straps, fixed axle to axle and called thoroughbraces.

And how many authors, writing of older times, employ the words *linsey-woolsey,* vaguely aware that it must have been shoddy stuff? It was a material of coarse wool, homespun, with linen its warp.

I often find muskets and rifles confused, whereas their only big similarity was that both were firearms. The inside of the barrel of the musket was smooth, that of the rifle spiraled with grooves. The grooves gave a spin to the bullet. Thus a musket ball slammed into the atmosphere while a bullet bored into it. The rifle was an accurate weapon, the musket unreliable. Unnecessary, this lore? Knowing details like these, I write with more surety, though it may not avail me otherwise.

It isn't in the historical novel alone that one finds indifference to or ignorance of fact. Contemporary fiction provides its own examples. A notable blunder is that of the northerner attempting the language of the South. He uses the terms *you all* and *y'all* when one person is talking to another. Now the terms mean "all of you." A southerner wouldn't think of saying "Y'all come back" to a single visitor on his departure.

It pays to know the language of your locality. I never heard a southern mountaineer use the word *expect.* Instead of saying, "I expect him home tomorrow," he would say, "I look for him home tomorrow." To that same man, to be afraid is to have the white eye, to lie sleepless the wide eye. In Kentucky I have never heard the word *guess* used except in the negative, as in "I don't guess so." Usually the word *reckon* is used in place of the positive *yes.*

In Boston and thereabouts, at least in the 1940s and perhaps today, a poached egg is a dropped egg. A milkshake of any flavor is a frap. It is common in the Boston area and perhaps elsewhere to add an *r* to words ending in a vowel or vowel sound. Thus a window becomes a "winder." In Cambridge I heard a radio entertainer sing, "The mere idear of you." Even President Kennedy had to watch out for that *r*. Strangely, that usually slighted letter is added in some parts of the Deep South. I've heard natives of the Pearl River country in Mississippi, speaking of Berea College in Kentucky, say "Berear."

In Vermont natives are likely to say when a storm is brewing, "Looks like we'll have some weather."

Foolish, this attention to speech? I don't think so. Used with care, such pecularities add to the verisimilitude of a story. Anyhow, they enchant me.

ELEVEN

Dialect

As you may make a character known by his speech, so will you bore the reader if you overdo it. In the beginning you may drop a few *g*'s, as indicated by apostrophes, and repeat the process sparingly later on, but the reader for the most part will drop them unconsciously once he knows the character's manner of speech. The apostrophe is used to show the elision of other letters, too, of course. I'm just saying that too many of them make a spiked and bothersome prose.

You may have your character say, "I never ever will do nothin' like that again." Thereafter be careful of overemphasis. Earlier Americans found it entertaining and funny to read a given character's style of speech, constantly repeated, even if a bit exaggerated. Here I'll quote from *Widow Bedott's Monologues* by Frances M. Whitcher as reprinted in *Blair's Early American Humor.*

> He was a wonderful hand to moralize, husband was, 'specially after he begun to enjoy poor health. He made an observation once when he was in one of his poor turns that I shall never forget the longest day I live. He says to me one winter evenin' as we was a-settin' by the fire, I was a-knittin' (I was always a wonderful great knitter)

and he was a smokin' (he was a master hand to smoke, though the doctor used to tell him he'd be better off to let tobacker alone; when he was well, used to take his pipe and smoke a spell after he'd got the chores done, and when he wa'nt well, used to smoke the biggest part o' the time). Well, he took the pipe out of his mouth and turned toward me. . . .

Ho hum.

TWELVE

Tenses and Voices

Sometimes you run onto a story written altogether in the present tense. Rarely is the method successful.

Let's say, "He goes to the door and hesitates, as if disaster may be waiting inside." Those words read like stage directions.

Make the sentence read, "He went to the door and hesitated, as if disaster maybe waited inside." By some unexplained process of mind the simple past tense conveys the impression of the present to the reader.

The constant repetition of the present tense becomes boring to the reader and, in my case at least, to the writer as well. For that reason I found screenwriting tedious. That demanded present tense all the time!

Large parts of Edward Abbey's *A Fool's Progress* are couched in the present tense, not with entire success. I have a suspicion he was trying to be different, trying too hard.

Use the past perfect, or pluperfect, tense as rarely as you can manage. One *had* ordinarily will suffice. It casts the reader back in time, as you wish, but too many *hads* keep reminding him that he is reading a digression or reversion from the present and so conduce to waning interest. After one past perfect verb form, you may slide into the simple past tense and give more life to your flashback.

Example:

He had rowed away from the island, leaving the boy. The boy stood at the edge of the water and shouted, waving a fist, "Come back, goddamn you! Come back!" By and by distance stilled the voice and dusk enveloped the boy.

The active voice is stronger than the passive voice.

And why is that? Simply because the active voice takes an object. It proceeds, subject, verb, object. The passive voice is slow and weak because it is reflective. It brings the reader back to the subject after the verb, a reversal of flow.

Example: "He hit the ball." (Direct and good.) "The ball was hit by him." (Not good. After the word *him* we have to reverse course to *the ball.*)

Which is not to say never use the passive voice. It has its uses and can be effective in some circumstances. Employ it advisedly, as an attorney might say.

THIRTEEN

Inert Material: Exposition

ANYTHING OFF THE STORY LINE constitutes what can be called inert material.

Exposition, explanation, description independent of your running narrative is inert. There it lies, an obstacle to the run of your story, a dam in the current.

And it is so easy to forget or ignore the simple fact that description of an object or process must be integrated with the story's movement.

An inert passage doesn't go anywhere. It exists all by itself, remote from character and action. It is off scene. Take Melville's *Moby-Dick.* Here is page after page of exposition as the author speaks at length of the ship and its components, their appearances and functions. To be sure, all this imparted knowledge comes in useful later on, but nevertheless it lies dead in the living story. It is as if Melville had taken time off from fiction to explain about the ship and its workings. He is preparing the reader for what is to come and being tedious in the process.

Could he have done better had he tried to integrate this information with the run of the story? Could he have done it?

Who knows?

Could I do it?

Don't even ask.

I have encountered problems of this kind, though they seem minor by comparison. In writing *The Big Sky* I had to deal with the ways by which men trapped beaver—where they set their traps, how they baited them, and with what and how did they kill their catches. Did they club the live animals in the traps or did they shoot them?

I had some personal knowledge about trapping in general, and I had done considerable research on the early-day trapping of beaver. I could have written directions, and that prospect was a temptation.

But how to incorporate that knowledge into the flow of the story? I knew one thing: I had to keep on scene.

So, keeping on scene, I had my trapper seek out the entrance to a beaver house or a customary landing stage and set his traps there. He baited each trap from a bottle of "medicine," carried on a string around his neck. The medicine, the contents of perineal glands of beaver, must have stunk to high heaven, but the mountain man was accustomed to stenches and the books don't mention it, so neither did I.

His trap set, my character led the chain out in the water and staked it there by means of a pole run through the ring of the chain and implanted in the stream bed. He knew that a beaver, caught in a trap, made for the water. There the weight of the trap would hold him down, and he would drown.

Here were all the techniques of trapping, exercised and observed by a live and active character.

I dare to think I avoided inertia.

Henry James wrote, "Show, don't tell." Here in three words he warns against inertia. Here is the difference between fiction and exposition. Of all the maxims it is the most difficult to observe all the time. In spite of yourself you may find you overlook the rule. Watch it!

FOURTEEN

Flashbacks: Backcasting

VERBS OF REMEMBERING and recollection are to be avoided. They yank the reader back a remove from the present. When I encounter a paragraph that begins "He remembered" or "In his recollection," I recoil. The writer may as well have said "He never would forget."

Ease the reader into your backcasts. A couple of examples:

> He felt a tug on the blanket and knew his mother was trying to rouse him. She was always gentle about it. She was, he thought, what people meant when they spoke of loving kindness. When he opened his eyes, her face would be over him, that fair and concerned face, framed by soft, brown hair. He waited as usual for his mother to put a hand on his forehead and smooth his hair back.
>
> But the blanket jerked hard, and he opened his eyes, and there was the bearded face of Old Dan, his whiskered lips saying, "Get up, kid. Time to eat a bait and git."

Or again:

> He sat idle, warmed by the fire, his drink on the chair arm, the first sips like a sleeping potion. He closed his

eyes, and there was her face again. She was smiling that good, hesitant smile of hers, and welcome shone in her eyes, and all he could say was "My dear. My dear." He was on his feet, his arms extended, and he kissed her and kissed her again and felt his blood warming, and again all he could say was "My dear."

A log fell in the fireplace, and he saw that the fire needed help, and he rose from his chair, careful not to spill the drink, and found another piece of wood and nestled it close against one almost burned out.

Fires needed a lot of attention.

FIFTEEN

Beginning Lines

An amusing, novel or challenging sentence can start a story on its way. Here are some examples:

"Take my camel, dear," said my aunt Dot as she climbed down from this animal on her return from High Mass.

—ROSE MACAULAY

He was born with the gift of laughter and a sense that the world was mad.   —RAFAEL SABATINI

I was on the outside of disaster, looking in. —DICK FRANCIS

I was squeezing a baseball when a loose-lipped character named Lancaster charged into the sheriff's office to report what he said was a murder.   —THE AUTHOR

Once there were three persons who met in the hospital and decided to live together. They arrived at this decision because they had no place to go when they were discharged.

—MARJORIE KELLOGG

Long ago a young reporter and I fell heir to a manuscript left on his death by a patient at an asylum for the mentally deranged. Its beginning read:

I was seventy-six years, three months, and five days
old when I was arrested as a timber thief.

Great stuff. A real hook of a beginning, but to our disap-
pointment the words that followed were tedious and unin-
spired.

A very good writer, a friend of mine, once was fumbling
for a beginning, a not infrequent problem of authors. His
story concerned an epileptic boy. The wisdom of the time said
his seizures were the work of the devil who had taken posses-
sion of his body. The cure called for a priest to beat the devil
out of the boy.

My friend had experimented with beginnings to no avail
and yet what if he had written . . .

"Lie still, my son," the priest said as he raised the whip.

Novel beginnings are easy to come by if thought about
idly without reference to text.

She said she would, but I didn't believe her, not until
next day. Then it was too late.

I told him the mountain was too tough. I warned him
against the windy, cloud-wrapped summit where uniden-
tified voices sounded. He laughed, and that was the last
I saw of him, alive, that is.

But be careful. You can overdo it and strain the reader's
credulity. And don't be upset if you can't come upon a novel
beginning. If your story is good, a clear beginning is enough.

SIXTEEN

Adjectives and Adverbs: Eager Enemies

MAXIM: The adjective is the enemy of the noun and the adverb the enemy of damn near everything else. Nouns and verbs are the guts of the language. That's another engraving for your skull.

The adjective, like the adverb, is insidious. It creeps in as helper for prose that is weak and makes it all the weaker.

William Saroyan, in a bit of satire, has written:

But rules without a system are, as every good writer will tell you, utterly inadequate. You can leave out "utterly" and the sentence will mean the same thing, but it is always nicer to throw in an "utterly" whenever possible. All successful writers believe that one word by itself hasn't enough meaning and that it is best to emphasize the meaning of one word with the help of another. Some writers will go so far as to help an innocent word with as many as four and five other words, and at times they will kill an innocent word by charity and it will take years and years for some ignorant writer who doesn't know adjectives at all to resurrect the word that was killed by kindness.

Long avoidance of adjectives and adverbs has led me to use them sparingly almost without thinking. Thus, writing recently about my view of the Rockies that rise four miles from my home, I wrote, "At sundown there will be a glory there."

With one noun, I thought later, I had achieved what an adjective or a string of them could not have.

As a further illustration of the value of nouns and verbs used almost alone, I go into nonfiction. I do so because the incident had a lasting influence on my life and work.

In my college days a professor asked us students to bring to class examples of prose we liked. I chose the opening lines of John Burroughs' *The Summit of the Years*. Here's a part of what I read.

> I am in love with this world. By my constitution I have nestled lovingly in it. It has been home. It has been my point of outlook into the universe. I have not bruised myself against it, nor tried to use it ignobly. I have tilled its soil, I have gathered its harvest, I have waited upon its seasons, and always have I reaped what I have sown. . . . I have climbed its mountains, roamed its forests, sailed its waters, crossed its deserts, felt the sting of its fronts, the oppression of its heats, the drench of its rains, the fury of its winds, and always have beauty and joy waited on my goings and comings.

Afterward the professor asked what made it good. None of us had a real or ready answer.

The instructor said then, "Note the few modifiers. Count the few adjectives and adverbs."

Before I bothered to count, a light began flickering in my head.

Perhaps I am being a bit too hard on adjectives and adverbs. Both have their uses.

Here's a home-grown example in which, it seems to me, both adverbs and adjectives serve well. Suppose in first-person fiction I write what is true of myself:

More and more, as I grew older, I was enchanted by the music of words. Even when I was a schoolboy there sounded, though faintly heard, the rhythm and tones of language. How wonderfully satisfying, I thought to myself as I worked, to make words sing and at the same time say what I wanted to say exactly as I wanted to say it. Was this something, I wondered, that Alfred North Whitehead was thinking about when he wrote that style was the ultimate morality of the mind?

SEVENTEEN

Plausibility

EDITH MERRILEES, a great teacher, once said, "Plausibility is the morality of fiction." And so it is.

If the reader doubts, if he thinks an incident, a development, a character's speech or reaction can't be real, then you have lost him or are about to lose him.

He will be suspicious if a character speaks or acts in a manner foreign to all he has been led to expect.

To avoid implausibility you must keep your descriptive words, your dialogue, and your internal monologue in harmony with the mental and educational planes of your characters. If you employ language foreign to them, whether in talk or description, the reader will pull back, thinking, not so, can't be.

If you choose to deal with the impossible, then start with an impossibility, as Kafka does in "The Prison Farm" and "The Metamorphosis." Then proceed, building on it. The narrative becomes a sort of fairy story, with overtones.

Another possibility, which does not dispute what has gone before. If one thing in your story is implausible, surround it with rock-hard nitty-gritty reality. Against such a credible background, the reader will come to accept it as the exception to the rule.

Think about your reader. Are you engaging or boring him? Does he believe or disbelieve? You are best served, it seems to me, especially if your background is alien, by a protagonist whose reactions resemble those natural to the reader. The protagonist is a surrogate. If the reader can cast your story aside and forget it, then you have failed.

EIGHTEEN

Coincidences

I T HAS BEEN SAID, rightly, that the reader will accept a coincidence if it aids the wrong party, not if it helps the right one.

The worn example of coincidence is that of the cavalry that arrives, unheralded, in the very nick of time. The reader will shake his head and think, "rigged deal." But if the besieging party, say a band of attacking Indians, is reinforced by unforeseen additions, the reader is not likely to be bothered.

But there are ways to turn coincidence into expectation. Suppose, early in the narrative, the commanding officer of the troops says to the wagon master, "We figure to be at the forks in ten days after scouting ahead. That's about when you should arrive. If we're not there, wait. You'll want our report." No surprise then if the cavalry shows up a little late. The tense question is, will it arrive in time?

In my Nieman year at Harvard, nine of us fellows attended a weekly seminar conducted by Theodore Morrison, hoping to improve our ability to communicate, to sharpen the very tool that was our livelihood. One of the men submitted a short story for general discussion. It involved a nighttime hold-up at a drug store, with a patrolman arriving when the robbery was in progress. It was a good story, marred by the officer's lucky arrival.

Morrison made a suggestion. The author went back to a time shortly before the hold-up and inserted lines somewhat like these:

> First clerk to a second one after a glance at the clock, "About time our friendly flatfoot showed up?"
>
> Second clerk, after himself consulting the clock, "Yep. Any time now. In this weather he'll be wanting his free Coke."

The story found an immediate buyer.

NINETEEN

Placing the Reader

THE READER WANTS to know where he is. That's to say, where your character or characters are. Outdoors or indoors? In a field where a cow may be grazing or on a busy city street? Is it night or day, dawn or dusk? Whereabouts on the map, unless that's already plain? If inside, where inside? In a hotel lobby, a residence, a room? Who's there, if anybody? What are the furnishings? Is the place hot or cold or neither? Is it welcoming? Forbidding?

As a writer you may tire of such details, but the reader won't. The more he knows about where he is, the more he'll be with you.

TWENTY

Rooting Interest

GIVE THE READER a rooting interest in your characters or character. Enlist him as their friend or their foe. Make him cheer or jeer, if silently. Interest him, involve his emotions in their fortunes, good or bad. Excite his concern with outcomes.

Without that rooting interest, without that concern, without that involvement, the reader may mutter, "So what?" He'll toss your story aside.

I recently read halfway through a novel in which the protagonist was an unlovely character for whom I wished neither ill fortune nor good. He was just a slob I didn't want to have around. I could find not one redeeming trait nor any real evil in the man. I gave the book away without finishing it.

For a while the cult of the antihero enjoyed considerable popularity. That popularity appears to be fading or to have faded, which is quite all right with me. Though its followers called it realism, it never was real and never could last.

These days there may be no men of fabled heroic stature, if ever there were, but there still exist men and women whose convictions and courage we can applaud—persons with at least some of the makings of heroes. And even in villains some trace of humanity abides.

In the late nineteen-thirties a man was hanged in my little hometown of Choteau, Montana. The punishment fit the crime, for he had killed the crippled operator of a very small subsistence stand and taken the thirty-five cents the till contained. At the end, with the rope around his neck, he pleaded, "Please don't let my mother know."

Such things are the stuff of fiction. Not the good and the bad set apart, but the mixture in all of us, varied in proportion from individual to individual.

For the purpose of fiction, its very necessity, is to give the reader a course of experience. Boring antiheroes, dull characters, and everyday routines won't take him on the journey.

TWENTY-ONE

Figures of Speech

I'M ALL FOR FIGURES OF SPEECH, provided only that they're not strained or overworked.

A strong wind is not so strong as a wind like a hand in your face.

The sun may shine hot, but it shines hotter if it shines hot as a blister or a torch.

I like Raymond Chandler's description of a detective. He says the man had a thumbnail like an ice cube. That simile told me the detective was a rough and unpleasant character as, indeed, he turned out to be.

Strunk and White in their *Elements of Style* advise caution in the use of figures of speech. Caution, yes. But don't be too cautious or you'll miss good chances for imagery.

I watch out for loose descriptions, abstractions, words of large embrace—which is to advise that you do, too. What does "beauty" mean or "beautiful" or "terrible" or "tragedy" or "ecstasy" or "magnificent"? Something, to be sure, and much sometimes. But illustrations and specifics are surer aids to ends.

TWENTY-TWO

Names

I ATTACH A GOOD DEAL of importance to the names I give my characters. Generally I use short ones for my more prominent personalities. Not always, though. When it came to a bookish man, I employed Collingsworth. It served, I thought, both as name and label.

More often, names like Mort or York or Jap or Burke occur to me.

It's best to avoid names that suggest each other or one another. Two names that begin with the same letter can be confusing. Samantha and Sarah, for instance. You might choose to avoid two names that suggest occupations, names like Mason and Carpenter.

Theodore Morrison believed that the letter "b" might be the boldest one in the alphabet. He used to quote, as a courageous and stubborn expression, the line from *MacBeth*, "We met them, daring, beard to beard, and beat them backward home."

It's your choice, though. You might consider that short names are easily remembered and their bearers quickly identified.

TWENTY-THREE

Novelty

E DMUND GOSSE, British writer and critic, once said, "The secret of successful fiction is a continual slight novelty."

The teasing of catch beginnings, given elsewhere in this manual, are marked by novelty. They succeed by it. It's what engages the reader. But don't overdo it. Remember it's fiction you're writing and not an example of your versatility.

I think of Larry McMurtry and his *Lonesome Dove.* As a longtime admirer of McMurtry, I dislike to fault his acclaimed book, but there it is, the novelty overdone. He has the camp cook tossing rattlesnake meat into the stew. Why, those young Texas cowpunchers would have killed a cook who did that. That's one example of excess novelty: I won't cite others.

A strangeness of feature, speech, or behavior on the part of a character will constitute novelty. An oddity of fact or lore may fit into your narrative, and it, too, will be novel.

But by far the greatest opportunity for novelty exists in your handling of language. Think of the best way of expressing a sentiment or presenting a situation. Often the best way is the novel way. In using it, you will avoid the prosaic. Your writing will be fresh and strong.

What might be called the misplaced modifier is an effective tool for novelty. I wrote once of "the breathless upthrust" of the Grand Tetons. I've read of beckoning distances and forlorn plains. I think of Gray's line, "The ploughman homeward plods his weary way."

The Tetons aren't breathless. The onlooker is. A country can't beckon or plains be forlorn. The ploughman is weary, not the way. Yet these misplaced modifiers do things that strict adherence to grammar can not. File them under novelty.

Finally, one sense can be employed to strengthen and enlarge the force of another. Kipling in his "Mandalay" has written, "An' the dawn comes up like thunder outer China 'crost the bay." And E. A. Robinson in "Dark Hills" wrote:

> Dark hills at evening in the West,
> Where sunset hovers like a sound
> Of golden horns . . .

Sound for sight, and sight all the better for it. There's Gosse's novelty.

TWENTY-FOUR

Overwriting

DON'T OVERWRITE. Choose your words. Make them work. Scratch the idlers. Beware of repetitious phrases. Beware of dialogue that is no more than chatter. Dialogue should forward the story.

Overwriting is the sin of most beginners, a sin into which even seasoned writers sometimes fall. It is as if the writer, doubtful of the reader's intelligence, were determined, by God, to make him understand by clubbing him with words.

Take a hunter who has climbed to his station in a tree beside a game trail that white-tail deer use on their way to water. He has made his way and climbed the tree by starshine, but, save for that feeble light, the night is still dark.

The hunter reports in the first person:

I seated myself as comfortably as I could and wondered how long until dawn. Already, in advance of the action, I felt my nerves tightening. It was always so. Expectation and hope began to beat in me, and I could feel the heart throb in the pads of my fingers. I fondled the rifle and breathed deep, hoping I wouldn't shake taking aim. The silent night closed in around me. I heard no bird calls, no squeaks or animals or flutter of leaves. I was alone, I and my nerves and the pulsing hope for the sight of an antlered buck on the trail. Breathe deep, man. Breathe deep. And keep it silent. Deer have ears. My own ears listened for footfalls. My eyes tried to pierce the crepuscular light. Any moment now. Any moment. I waited, my every sense keen and alert, my every nerve drawn tight as a bowstring.

Enough of that junk. How often do we, the readers, need to be told the man was nervous? At the end we've been dinned into total indifference.

If, having established himself in the tree in the dark and quiet night, we have the hunter say, "I felt the old hunting excitement stirring in my blood. My hands would steady once I had game in my sights. The feel of the rifle reassured me. It wouldn't, it couldn't be long now. I breathed the silence and waited for the world to wake up."

Point made?

TWENTY-FIVE

Verbs of Saying

OGS BARK. Men don't. Yet how often does one encounter something like this: "He barked, 'No, I will not!'" I sometimes read "He hissed" when there is no "s" sound in the quotation. No one can hiss "I wouldn't do that." Smiles and snarls and grunts don't utter words. It is people who do that. People say or ask or reply. These are verbs of saying.

As advised earlier, don't fear to write "said." The repetition of it may pall on you, but the reader won't notice. The whole purpose of the "he said" or "she said" or "Gene said" is to identify the speaker.

All those smiles and snarls and grunts are meant to suggest mood, whereas the words said, the words within quotations, should suggest or imply the mood.

Adverbs that modify verbs of saying can be ludicrous. "'Go to hell, you bastard,' he said angrily." Now who wouldn't have thought the speaker was angry?

TWENTY-SIX

False Leads

DON'T AROUSE EXPECTATIONS and then forget them.

Same advice in other words: Do not introduce an interesting cast and situation early on and lose them as your story proceeds.

You'll leave the reader asking, "What happened to those people? How did things turn out? Whose story is this, anyway? What is this story about?"

A dissatisfied reader makes a poor fan.

Again the easiest illustration comes from my own work. In *These Thousand Hills* I made a solid and interesting character of Ram Butler, the trail boss of a crew driving cattle from Oregon to Montana. A few chapters later, I left him, left him for good, left him because I didn't know what more to do with him or with members of the crew save for my protagonist and his pal.

But in attention to Butler, in making him a character one wanted to follow, I overdid it. The consequence was that readers asked me, "What ever happened to that man Butler? You never told us."

There was a false lead, not in the direction of the story as I saw it but in the making and then the abandonment of a man in whom I had created too much interest.

So I learned a lesson, not the first or the last, by any tally.

TWENTY-SEVEN

The Obligatory Scene

THE PHRASE may need some definition.

The obligatory scene is the scene you have been preparing the reader for. It is the scene he has been led to expect from conversations, conflicts, and episodes. It is a resolution, one that may not be pleasing but is satisfying in that it answers the reader's expectations.

When you come to that scene, for goodness' sake, write it without evasion or delay. Because it may deal with what is brutal, nasty, offensive, and difficult to handle, some authors skip over it, backcasting later in a tame paragraph or two.

Other writers, up against this obligation, choose to digress before tackling it. Even as respected an author as Saul Bellow sometimes indulges in paragraph after paragraph of recollection, while the reader prays he'll get down to business. Too much of that sort of thing is, well, too much.

Plunge in.

TWENTY-EIGHT

Profane and
Barnyard Words

IN OUR PERMISSIVE SOCIETY the raw and vulgar words are being accepted more and more and used in social conversation by both men and women with a freedom that would have shocked older generations. That doesn't call for their overuse in fiction. Bernard DeVoto once said one goddamn on a page was worth a hundred and a hundred were worth nothing.

Advice: Use the four-letter words only when they seem the only right ones, the words that your character would use, or else seem out of character. And then employ them sparingly.

More than one novel has been spoiled by reliance on what we used to call smut. Writers who repeatedly use it may do so for shock effect, but their very frequency dulls any shock. It becomes tiresome.

I don't like gutter talk, yet I know full well that words are only sounds made by mouth and tongue, in themselves innocent. It is only our added implications that make them clean or dirty. And what is smut in one language, as well as what is sacrilegious, may be quite acceptable in another. Many a Mexican boy and man has Jesús as a given name.

TWENTY-NINE

Rewriting

Some established writers have stated they never rewrite but have said what they wish to say in the way they wish in their first drafts. Maybe so, but I doubt you will be among the chosen. I'm not.

It is an exaggeration to report that I wrote the first chapter of one of my novels thirteen times, for in the rewriting I used substantial parts of what I had typed before, but I did fuss with that chapter thirteen times.

So don't shrink from revisions. Your first draft before you, you are likely to think of amendments, additions, and improvements that had not occurred to you. Your imagination takes flight, your interest soars. Ah, now, that's better. That's just fine. Here I go.

But hold on a minute. When I speak of first drafts, I am referring to a just-written rough chapter or paragraph, not to changes necessitated by the further development of your story. Maybe an early character has altered in age, temperament, or outlook . . . maybe an earlier incident needs amendment. But do not, repeat do not, interrupt your progress by halting and turning back to make the changes. Proceed to the end of your novel and then do the fixing. To do otherwise is to risk losing purpose, enthusiasm, and momentum. Carl Brandt, literary agent, puts it this way:

> I have seen far too many novels and even some nonfiction work shrivel and die because the authors insisted on going back and rewriting earlier chapters to conform to changes that might occur midway through. They do go back, they do make the changes, and by the time they get back up to where they left off, the fire in the belly that led to those particular middle chapters has somehow been altered or changed.
>
> I do tell my clients, particularly the younger ones, that they should work their way through a complete first draft even if their 45-year-old hero has become a 25-year-old heroine somewhere around chapter 6.

Once a beginning writer asked me to criticize his full-length manuscript, a thing I won't do any more. His work had promise. So much promise that I made a long list of suggested improvements, feeling the manuscript was close to publishable. He just had to spend more time on it.

Three months after I had submitted my list, I saw him again and asked about his progress. "Oh," he said, "that." He waved it away. "I haven't had time for it. I'm almost finished with a new novel."

None of his work has ever seen print.

THIRTY

The Elusive Theme

IT SEEMS TO ME that every good story has a theme, recognized or not. Tell your story and don't worry. The theme lies in it, maybe to be discovered by critics, not by you.

In "Barn Burning" was Faulkner thinking of the impotence of good against evil or of decency against vulgarity? I think I would guess not.

And what might have been his theme in "A Rose for Emily"? You guess. I'm sure that wasn't Faulkner's concern. He had a story to tell.

What was Hemingway's purpose in writing "The Capital of the World"? To write effectively, of course, and just perhaps in the conviction that it was better to die young, life being what it was.

What's the theme in that fine movie *Tunes of Glory?* Perhaps turns of loyalty says it, but I question whether that was first in the makers' minds.

Themes are critics' concerns, not necessarily yours.

THIRTY-ONE

Writing like Others

Y OU MAY WANT TO IMITATE some admired author. That's all right within limits. It's altogether likely, in following someone else's manner you will develop your own, as published authors have done.

If you want to write like Faulkner or Joyce or Henry James or Ernest Hemingway or any of those writers whom *The New Yorker* likes, go ahead. In all probability you will develop your own style in trying to ape them.

William Saroyan has something to say on this subject:

Someone who isn't a writer begins to want to be a writer and he keeps on wanting to be one for ten years, and by that time he has convinced all his relatives and friends and even himself that he is a writer, but he hasn't written a thing and he is no longer a boy, so he is getting worried. All he needs now is a system. Some authorities claim there are as many as fifteen systems, but actually there are only two: (1) you can decide to write like Anatole France or Alexandre Dumas or somebody else, or (2) you can decide to forget that you are a writer at all and you can decide to sit down at your typewriter and put words on paper, one at a time, in the best fashion you know how.

THIRTY-TWO

Two Exercises

H ERE ARE TWO SUGGESTED EXERCISES, the only ones we'll propose. If others occur to you, fine.

Write a love scene without using the word *love* or any synonym.

Write a scene of angry confrontation without using the word *anger* or anything close to it such as *rage.*

Let's have a go now at a love scene.

They fell silent, holding hands. He felt the warmth of her clasp, and it seemed to him, here in the wordless quiet with night closing in on the high plains, that the secret of life was almost revealed. Her hand, her dear hand. What was it some poet had said, "a woman of itself"? Marvell? No. Browning, yes Browning, speaking of Andrea del Sarto, holding the hand of his mistress. He felt the pressure of her hand as it answered to his own. Yes, a woman of itself.

THIRTY-THREE

Easy
on the Wisdom

WHATEVER WISDOM a writer has exists, or should exist, in dispersion, in the responses of his characters, in their reactions and language, in the turns of the plot.

Too often the novice throws in chunks of philosophy, of learned attitude and truly wonderful thinking, this to impress the reader and prove his claim to authorship. What these indigestible outpourings do is stand in the way of the story. They are inert and out of place and prove only that the beginner is a beginner.

Similarly, what the beginning writer most prizes, the passages he considers most elegant and striking and deeply affecting, probably should come out. They're likely just overblown prose, standing unconnected and awkward, standing like dams in the stream of narrative.

Mack, a character in Steinbeck's *Sweet Thursday,* has this to say in the prologue:

Sometimes I want a book to break loose with a bunch of hooptedoodle. The guy's writing it, give him a chance to do a little hooptedoodle. Spin up some pretty words maybe, or sing a little song with language. That's nice, but I wish it was set aside so I don't have to read it. I don't want hooptedoodle to get mixed up in the story. So if the guy that's writing it wants hooptedoodle, he ought to put it right at first. Then I can skip it if I want to, or maybe go back to it after I know how the story comes out.

As it is the tendency of the beginner to write chunks of indigestible wisdom, so it is his tendency to parade big words. He may fall in love with such polysyllables as concatenation or supposititious or animadversion, and trot them out to prove he knows his stuff. What they prove is that he has some acquaintance with some long words. Now these are perfectly good words, and there may come a time when their use is called for. Usually, when you are about to use such a word, it is better to look for a simpler one that conveys the same meaning, or two simple words perhaps. If these escape you, consult your thesaurus. That's what it's for.

Thoreau said, "Simplify, simplify, simplify." He was speaking of a way of life, of course, but the advice has some application to fiction.

THIRTY-FOUR

Authors and Alcohol

I HAVE HEARD writers say they do their best work when drinking or drunk. I don't believe them.

Raymond Chandler is reported to have said he couldn't find an ending to one of his excellent stories unless he took time to get drunk.

Up to a point I accept that report. For alcohol can stimulate imagination. It can find inventions. But I'll lay my bottom dollar, as one not unacquainted with booze, that Chandler had to sober up to write that ending.

My experience is that even one drink diminishes the ability to write well. The brute fact is that too many authors have drunk themselves out of production and too many into the graveyard.

THIRTY-FIVE

Talking a Story
to Death

THE TROUBLE WITH WRITERS' colonies as I know them is talk. Here the brethren come, full of themselves, each full of enthusiasm for the work he is going to write and can't wait to get around to. He can't wait, either, to explain his great idea to his fellows. So he tells them and tells them, waiting with some impatience while they take their ebullient turns.

He goes on day by day, telling his story idea over and over again until it stales in his mind. Each telling has diminished his inner impetus, has worn away at his first fine urge to put words on paper. "Well," he says to himself then, "I guess my idea wasn't too good in the first place. I'll get a new inspiration, soon." And never, in all that time, has he written a fresh word. Coroner's verdict: Death by gabble.

The professional writer talks little about his project or projects. He may name the general subject, report how he's getting along, and that's it. He saves his words for paper.

THIRTY-SIX

Critics:
Uncle Joe Liked It

HIS STORY FINISHED (he thinks), the tyro is likely to show it around, to friends, kinsmen, and other beginners, asking for their honest opinions though what he wishes for is praise. Praise raises his spirits. It bolsters his faith. It is his certificate of authorship.

He forgets or ignores that the comments he gets are those of uninformed critics, who usually are too kindly to speak ill of his manuscript even though they might dislike it.

What should the beginners do then? Find a man or woman, if he can, whose judgment is professional and whose word he respects. Find one such critic (no easy task) or possibly two but no more and listen. Listen!

Too many appraisals, even by independent professionals or publishers' editors, can be fatal. If a manuscript is good but maybe not quite good enough, the author may send it to publisher after publisher. He'll get a variety of suggestions for improvement, probably. If he tries to satisfy all of them, he is likely to wind up with nothing. One woman I know did just that. She wrote and rewrote, heeding editorial opinions. Her final version was far from as good as the original story. To my knowledge it never was published.

Perhaps she should have had more confidence in herself. Writing always comes down to yourself, to your best judgment. If critics have a good point, heed them. If not, then ignore them. An absence of confidence is a sure way to a mess. But supreme confidence, the conviction you stand above all suggestions, is just as bad. You'll wind up then with a trunkful of rejected manuscripts.

Possibility: If a school near you conducts a writers' workshop, you might see about joining. In such a program, directed by a teacher, students submit their work for general discussion. Here, in considering the efforts of others, you will apply a critical faculty that disappears when you try to appraise your own. In the process you may learn, by osmosis, to bring that same faculty to bear on what you have done.

THIRTY-SEVEN

Authors and Agents

O NLY BY LIBERAL ALLOWANCE does the matter of agents get a place in this manual. But because the question most often asked of authors by would-be authors is "How do I get an agent?" I'll tell how, kind of.

The beginner finds himself in a Catch-22 situation. It is difficult to get an agent without having been published: it is difficult to find a publisher for unagented copy.

Sometimes, if rarely, the intercession of a knowledgeable friend who knows the agent will work.

If the novice sends in an arresting manuscript, one that may not be publishable but portends other and better ones, then he just may be successful, but don't bet the farm on it.

Generally, I think the best procedure is to send a sample of your writing to the agent you've selected and with that, a covering letter. Now bear in mind that the letter is very important. An agent wants to know about you, about what you've done, and about the work you want to do. What are your ambitions? Go ahead. Spill it. He wants to know. He is interested in long-term associations.

Beware of agents who advertise and charge reading fees. Reputable agents do no such things. They operate solely on the ten or fifteen percent commission they charge for copy that is sold. That's what makes them so choosy. Why waste money and effort sending unsalable stuff to publishers?

I acquired my first agent through the intercession of a friend. The agent was Maxwell Aley, and he found a publisher for my first book, a poor thing, as I believe I have said.

With Mr. Aley's death and the publication of *The Big Sky*, I needed representation, so I went in person to the offices of Brandt and Brandt in New York. The elder Carl Brandt, father of the present one, received me amiably and said sure and welcome. I had an agent as of then.

I've been a thankful client in all the years since.

Why have an agent beyond the immediate advantages I have mentioned? Why am I thankful? Answer: An agent knows the markets. He also knows contracts, and he watches out for a client in all the proposals the client receives. He is the author's guide, promoter, and guardian.

THIRTY-EIGHT

Getting to Work

Y OU DON'T WANT to sit down and write. What a dreary prospect, sitting there alone, trying to put words on paper, trying for the right words, avoiding the easy and careless expressions. Better to take out the garbage or even write checks against the monthly bills. You have nothing in your head anyway.

So you put other things first. You dawdle. You work a puzzle or mow the lawn or talk prices with your spouse and, first thing you know, it's time for an appointment or a trip to school for the kids. Hell, the sun is over the yardarm now. Time for a drink. So the day passes, empty, and you go to bed feeling worthless. You tell yourself you ought to rent a garret somewhere, but the fault lies not with your surroundings but with you.

How familiar I am with this dismal scene.

In a long experience I have found many ways that help.

Tell yourself, "All right, I don't feel like working, but I can work just half an hour and then call it quits." But you'll get interested, and time will go on and the half hour will be multiplied.

Make yourself sit down before a typewriter or pen. You can do that much, can't you, even if you don't put a line on paper? Well, maybe a line. In any case, sitting down at the desk is the first and necessary step in a day's work.

As a stimulant you may retype the last page of the work done yesterday and thus find your imagination awakened.

Now, if you have had a decent day, it may be well to quit though you want to go on. You'll be encouraged next day to proceed with what you left undone.

Be reconciled. I don't find actual writing any fun. There is mere tedium in typing words. But the fun comes, the great reward comes, when you have written a line, a paragraph, or a chapter that strikes you just right.

Once I spent half a day on two lines of dialogue, but finally got them to please me and so felt good.

For ease in writing you should have the right appurtenances—good light, a chair that suits you, a table or desk of the right height, copy paper, pens, pencils, or typewriter, according to habit and choice. A table of dining-table height may suit the hand but is too tall for easy typewriter operation. For working drafts I use yellow copy paper. When I am satisfied with what I've done, I go to a professional typist who prepares the publisher's manuscript. Remember to have a copy made for your files. The cost of copying varies from place to place but should be no more than ten cents a page.

You'll need a good, unabridged dictionary. In the course of the years I've accumulated four, but rely for the most part on just one.

And you'll need a thesaurus. I always resort to my Roget's, published in 1922. There are numerous later thesauruses, of which I have two or three, but I always consult my first love.

The thing is to use the aids you are comfortable with. If you feel better writing in longhand, do so. If you have gone modern—modern to me may be old hat to you—and like working with a word processor, fine. Why not? Call it an idiosyncrasy or a crotchet, but I go along with a portable, manual typewriter. Friends have smiled at me, and I smile at myself but stay faithful to Smith-Corona, unelectrified. I know how to spell and don't need a machine to tell me what's right.

If you are shaky as to the accepted and correct usage of words, then go out and get Strunk and White's *The Elements of Style* immediately. It deals with accepted usage, punctuation, clarity, and much more, and is by far the best book of its kind.

If it is beyond you, if you have to go back to basic grammar, parts of speech, and all that, then God be with you. You'll need Him.

THIRTY-NINE

Maxims
and Counsels

H ERE IS THE ADVICE I try to follow:

"Show, don't tell." —HENRY JAMES

"The object of the novelist is to keep the reader entirely oblivious of the fact that the author exists—even of the fact he is reading a book." —FORD MADOX FORD

"Any work of art must first of all tell a story." —ROBERT FROST

"Plausibility is the morality of fiction." —EDITH MERRILEES

"The secret of successful fiction is a continual slight novelty." —EDMUND GOSSE

.   .   .

Good enough is never good enough. The very best you can do may be good enough.

The adjective is the enemy of the noun and the adverb the enemy of the verb, the adjective, and the adverb itself.

The task of fiction is to excite, not imprison, the imagination of the reader. So watch those adjectives.

Unlike expository writing, good fiction sticks to characters, their actions, speech, and thought. It stays on scene.

If you switch viewpoint, make it plain early on that a different character has taken over.

The good writer keeps asking himself, "What am I doing to the reader?"

Write a good scene and much else will be forgiven you.

The good writer makes every word count.

Showing opens doors: telling closes them.

Give the reader a rooting interest—or lose him.

Question yourself if you are leaving your character to solitary musings.

Don't be funny-funny. "Sez" for "says" is about as funny as a migraine.

A writer's wisdom exists in dispersion.

If you have a good story to tell, then tell it. Introductions such as "I never will forget" are fatal.

Don't overdo figures of speech. Don't get cute.

Take care with the past perfect tense and the passive voice.

The good writer takes the reader on a course of experience.

Lose yourself in your characters and they may emerge large as life.

As a writer of fiction you will skirt the edges of sentimentality. Don't shrink but don't fall in.

FORTY

The Writer's Morality

THE WRITER MUST ENTERTAIN, else his manuscripts will molder on the shelf, written but unsung. He should also shed at least a ray of light on human experience, on the human condition. These are his moralities, entertainment and illumination, enforced by the high resolve to write his best.